POSH PROTOCOL Volume III

~

PRAYERS OF THE KINGDOM HEIR

POSH PROTOCOL Volume III

~

PRAYERS OF THE KINGDOM HEIR

C. C. Preston ● Dr. Posh ®

Copyright © 2021

Copyright © 2021 C.C. Preston, Dr. Posh® All rights reserved. Author Photos Purchased. Printed in the United States. No part of this book may be used or reproduced in any form or manner without written permission, except in the case of brief quotations embodied in articles and reviews.

ISBN 10: 1-7376096-0-5
ISBN 13: 978-1-7376096-0-5

TO

The Holy Spirit,

I Love You

CONTENTS

Prayers of the Kingdom Heir   1

Prayer of Deliverance   5

Praying in Tongues   11

Prayer of Love   15

Prayer of Liberty   19

Prayer of Restoration   23

Prayer of Promotion   27

CONTENTS

Prayer of Expansion   31

Prayer of Dominion   35

Prayer of Business Ownership   39

Prayer of Wealth Building   43

Prayer of Favor & Influence   47

Prayer of Salvation   55

ACKNOWLEDGMENTS

Giving Honor and Thanks to my Lord and Savior Jesus Christ.

I am nothing without you Lord.

Our Always Prayer

Abba Father,
Endow us with the knowledge, wisdom and power to always be a Representation of You.

We Love You, Always.

In the Name of Jesus, Amen

"But ye shall receive power, after that the Holy Ghost is come upon you. . ."
(Acts 1:8, King James Version)

Prayers

of the

Kingdom Heir

The Holy Bible actually tells us how to pray. God loves us so much that he has provided us with the exact method as to how we are to pray. It is found in Matthew 6:9-13 "After this manner therefore pray ye: Our Father which art in heaven, Hallowed be thy name. Thy kingdom come. Thy will be done in earth, as *it is* in heaven. Give us this day our daily bread. And forgive us our debts, as we forgive our debtors. And lead us not into temptation, but deliver us from evil: For thine is the kingdom, and the power, and the glory forever." Amen

We are also told how much to pray in 1 Thessalonians 5:17 which directs us to "Pray without ceasing." Prayer is how we converse with Elohim, our Heavenly Father, and the only true and living God. Prayer should be so natural to us that when we don't pray we immediately become aware of the increased distance between us and our Heavenly Father.

As Heirs to the Kingdom of God, it is imperative that we talk to God, all day every day. Let's talk to God when we rise in the morning, all throughout our day and as we prepare to end our day with rest. We often ask God for specific things in our prayers but it is ok to just have a general conversation with God without submitting a request.

Additionally, we sometimes miss one of the most important aspects of prayer, and that is pausing in our conversation with God, so that he can speak to us. Prayer is not a one-way conversation. God has something to tell us. Spend time with him listening to his instructions. I assure you they are life changing.

Listening for and obeying the voice of God requires faith. "Now faith is the substance of things hoped for, the evidence of things not seen." Hebrews 11:1. It's impossible to please God without faith. Hebrews 11:6

Prayer of Deliverance

The Holy Trinity is God the Father, God the Son and God the Holy Spirit, three manifestations of the one and only living God. Jesus the Son, died in our stead on the cross to restore our relationship with God the Father and in doing so we can now live for eternity in heaven through Salvation.

John 3:16 tells us "For God so loved the world, that he gave his only begotten Son, that whosoever believeth in him should not perish, but have everlasting life." Jesus is our only way to the Father (John 14:6), and as such, we are to pray to the Father "in the Name of Jesus." This is confirmed in John 14:13-14 where Jesus tells us "And whatsoever you ask in my name, that, I will do, that the Father may be glorified in the Son. If you ask anything in my name, I will do it." As we begin to talk to God in prayer, we will preface or conclude each prayer by saying "in the Name of Jesus."

In the Name of Jesus, in this prayer of deliverance, I take authority over, renounce and break every word curse and deed curse of failure, poverty, lack, debt, silence, premature death, destruction, accidents, sickness, illness, mental illness, double-mindedness, perpetual singleness, divorce, anxiety and addiction that has ever been pronounced over my life or my bloodline. I take authority over, renounce and break every word curse and deed curse of witchcraft, occult or satanic activity that has ever been pronounced over my life or my bloodline. Amen

In the Name of Jesus, I take authority over, renounce and break every word curse and deed curse of fear, confusion, trickery, deception, despair, sullenness, self-hatred, self-sabotage, wandering, pride, bitterness, rebellion, torment and oppression that has ever been pronounced over my life or my bloodline. Amen

The Power of Praying in your Heavenly Language

Praying in Tongues

Speaking or praying in tongues is a heavenly language that allows our spirit to converse directly with the Holy Spirit. This spiritual gift is a source of nutrition and edification for our spirit. By speaking and praying in tongues our spirit will grow strong and we will begin to operate in an elevated level of supernatural power and revelation.

If you do not yet have the gift of speaking and praying in tongues and would like to have this gift, pray the following prayer, Holy Spirit manifest your power within me and create in me a unique heavenly language through which my spirit will communicate directly with you. As my spirit grows closer to you through our daily talks, open my eyes to miracles and supernatural occurrences while increasing my discernment and downloading supernatural revelation into my spirit. In the Name of Jesus, Amen

After you have received the gift of speaking and praying in tongues, set a goal for yourself that you will use your heavenly language 1 to 2 hours per day. This goal does not have to be accomplished all at once. Use your heavenly language consistently throughout your entire day. Pair the use of your heavenly language with other activities you are engaged in such as while you work, garden, cook, etc.

Use your heavenly language as you engage in all of your activities of daily living. The word of God tells us in 1 Corinthians 14:40 to "Let all things be done decently and in order." Use a low and slow voice tone when necessary to ensure that you are observing and adhering to the protocol of the environment you are in.

Speak in tongues and pray in tongues as much as you possibly can. You will establish a close relationship with the Holy Spirit that will change your life forever.

Prayer of Love

As a Kingdom Heir, Jesus states "Thou shalt love the Lord your God with all your heart, with all your soul, and with all your mind. This is the first and greatest commandment. And the second is like it: Love your neighbor as yourself." Matthew 22:37-39. We are the mirror image of God and as such, we are to give back to God what he gives us. "We love him, because he first loved us." 1 John 4:19. Let's Pray!

Father God, in the Name of Jesus, I pray that your love will radiate through me and touch the lives of people in such a way that they seek out a closer relationship with you. "Let the words of my mouth, and the meditation of my heart, be acceptable in they sight, O LORD, my strength, and my redeemer." Psalm 19:14. Lord, as I walk through life and generously extend your love to others, I pray for the vision and wisdom to recognize and receive genuine love from others. Amen

Abba Father, I pray for the strength, tenacity, willpower and courage to choose love over fear. I pray that love, along with your word, will always be the dominant focus of my life's work and the decisions I make. Lord let love prevail in my mind, body and soul. Let love win over worry, doubt and indecisiveness. Let love have free reign in my ministry and in my business. Lord, let love survive within me through trials, tragedy and even triumphs.

    Father God, I thank you for creating me in your very own image as your Daughter and Heir to your Kingdom. I thank you for loving me so much that you sent your Son Jesus to die on the cross for me so that I could be free and reconciled to you. Lord, I thank you for your grace and mercy. "O give thanks unto the LORD; for *he is* good; for his mercy endureth for ever." 1 Chronicles 16:34 Amen

Prayer of Liberty

As Kingdom Heirs, we have been set free, Hallelujah! "Stand fast therefore in the liberty wherewith Christ hath made us free, and be not entangled again with the yoke of bondage." Galatians 5:1. As a Kingdom Heir, embrace and proclaim your freedom. "Let the redeemed of the LORD say so, whom he hath redeemed from the hand of the enemy;" Psalm 107:2. Let's Pray!

    Heavenly Father, in the Name of Jesus, I pray that I will continue to walk in the freedom you have provided for me. I pray that I will never lose sight of the gift of liberation from condemnation, that I have been given through Jesus Christ. I pray that my mind will remain free from the deceptions, entanglements and false accusations of the enemy. I pray that my thoughts, hopes and dreams will be forever free of stress and worry. I pray that my thoughts will be forever focused on you Lord. Amen

Father God, I thank you for sending your Son Jesus Christ to die for the remission of my sins, which freed me from the punishment that I deserve. I thank you that I have been given everlasting life through the shed blood of the lamb. "Herein is love, not that we loved God, but that he loved us, and sent his Son *to be* the propitiation for our sins." 1 John 4:10.

Abba Father, I thank you that "the Spirit of the Lord GOD is upon me; because the LORD hath anointed me to preach good tidings unto the meek; he hath sent me to bind up the brokenhearted, to proclaim liberty to the captives, and the opening of the prison to them that are bound;" Isaiah 61:1.

Lord, I thank you that I am free to walk out the plans that you have for my life, my ministry and my business without regret. I thank you that I am free to live the life you have created just for me. Amen

Prayer of Restoration

As a Kingdom Heir, if you have suffered an emotional or physical injury, illness or loss in any area of your life (most of us have), freely pray to God for restoration. "Ask and it will be given to you; seek and you will find; knock and the door will be opened to you." Matthew 7:7. Know that our God is willing and able to restore you to the *version of you*, he created you to be. Let's pray!

Heavenly Father, in the Name of Jesus, I pray for the healing and restoration of my mind, body and soul. I pray to be healed, restored and made whole from all the traumas, illnesses and injuries I have experienced throughout my entire life, no matter how small or how large they may be.

I pray for the restoration of my self-esteem, self-worth and self-value. I pray my view of myself will be restored to reflect your view of me and I pray I will fully embrace the newly restored me. Amen

Abba Father, in the Name of Jesus, I pray for the restoration of healthy relationships with family members and friends. I pray for the restoration of healthy channels of communication to nurture and grow these relationships. I pray for the restoration of my ability to express my true thoughts and emotions.

I pray for the restoration of all of the hopes and dreams I once had for my life that were abandoned due to the challenges of everyday living. I pray for the restoration of the desire to pursue the new hopes and dreams you have placed within me.

I pray for the restoration of the assets, wealth and opportunities that I missed, squandered or lost. I pray for the restoration of every good thing that I didn't receive because I was out of your will or in a state of rebellion and I pray for the restoration of the assets, wealth and opportunities that were wrongfully taken from me. Amen

Prayer of Promotion

As Kingdom Heirs, we are not to be fearful when asking God to promote us. The Bible speaks to us concerning fear in Luke 12:32, "Fear not, little flock, for it is your Father's good pleasure to give you the kingdom." Not only are we not to be fearful, we must know, God takes pleasure in giving us our abounding Kingdom inheritance. Let's pray!

Abba Father, in the Name of Jesus, I pray for promotion in the areas of ministry, service and leadership. I pray to be promoted within ministry so that my ministerial voice is elevated and the message of the Gospel of Jesus Christ is broadcast to the Nations.

I pray to be promoted within the area of service as it relates to ministerial participation such as preaching and volunteering. I pray to be promoted within the area of service within my global community by educating and empowering the members of the community. Amen

Father God, I pray for promotion in the areas of self-development and self-discipline. I pray to be promoted to a higher level of understanding of the personal development that I need. I pray for promotion in the area of leadership including team leadership and organizational leadership.

I pray for promotion in the area of leadership as it relates to teaching, mentoring and leading others in developing the highest and best version of themselves. I pray for promotion in the area of leading by example. I pray to be promoted to new and challenging leadership roles within ministry and within business.

Abba Father, thank you for answered prayers. I thank you for the growth, maturity and strength that will accompany my promotion. I thank you that my promotion will lead to the promotion of others in your Kingdom. Amen

Prayer of Expansion

As Kingdom Heirs, God wants to expand us with the oil of the anointing so that his Kingdom will expand. God wants to expand us globally. His word reveals this to us in Mark 16:15, where he tells us to "Go into all the world and preach the gospel to every creature." His desire for us is to have a global reach with our voice and our actions. Let's pray!

Heavenly Father, in the Name of Jesus, please expand the reach of my voice. May my voice travel throughout the entire world presenting the Good News of the Gospel. Expand the capacity of my mind to ingest more of your word so that it can be released through me to the far reaches of the earth. Take my voice, filled with your word, to places where people do not know your name and do not have access to a Bible. I pray that you expand the work of discipleship within your Kingdom Heirs. Transform us into living epistles. Amen

Abba Father, expand the reach of my actions in the global business and ministry marketplace. May my strategic actions in ministry and in business take me to environments, rooms and tables where blessing upon blessing and miracle upon miracle are awaiting my arrival. Activate my actions with purpose, plans and positioning to teach, build, prosper and grow.

Father God, I pray that you will expand me in the areas of my life where my self-development is key to my global outreach. I pray for emotional and intellectual expansion. Unveil yourself to me in ways that expand my ability to learn more about who you are and how much you love me. Expand my ability to overcome doubt and fear. Help me to believe that with you, anything is possible. Your word tells us in Mark 9:23 "…If thou canst believe, all things are possible to him that believeth." Amen

Prayer of Dominion

As Kingdom Heirs, it has been Gods desire from the very beginning that we have dominion here on the earth. Genesis 1:26 "And God said, Let us make man in our image, after our likeness: and let them have dominion over the fish of the sea, and over the fowl of the air, and over the cattle, and over all the earth, and over every creeping thing that creepeth upon the earth." We must remember to operate in dominion. Let's pray!

Heavenly Father, in the Name of Jesus, I pray for the courage to walk in the authority that you have already given to me. I pray for the courage to exercise dominion over the territory that you have set me in and assigned to me. I pray for dominion in areas that have been particularly targeted by the lies and works of satan. I pray that you would send your word through your Kingdom Heirs to these areas to speak life and liberty to those held captive by satans deception. Amen

Father God, I pray for the tenacity, strength and wisdom to dominate in the business marketplace. I pray for fearlessness and extremely effective leadership abilities in the business marketplace. I pray my words, products and services will dominate in the global marketplace. I pray the authority my business carries will always be a continual representation of your love for me.

Abba Father, your word says in Matthew 10:16, "Behold, I send you out as sheep in the midst of wolves; so be shrewd as serpents and innocent as doves." I pray for the ability to be so shrewd in ministry and in business that my negotiated monetary and service contracts will result in the supernatural manifestation of exponential favor and increase for me in the form of cash, electronic income deposits, stocks, bonds, commercial real estate and residential real estate, domestically and internationally. Amen, it is so!

Prayer of Business Ownership

As Kingdom Heirs, we are to prosper as our soul prospers, 3 John 1:2. One of the ways in which we can do this is by being business owners. While business ownership can be daunting and challenging, the rewards of it are Kingdom based. As the seed of entrepreneurship is planted within us and begins to sprout, we must remember the source. Let's pray!

Abba Father, in the Name of Jesus, I pray for the seed of entrepreneurship along with ingenious ideas, visions and inventions. I pray for unique opportunities to prosper through successful business ownership. I pray for my businesses to grow locally and expand globally. I pray for global business influence and success. I pray for favorable outcomes in business marketing, promotion and advertisement. I pray for the global success and recognition of all my brands, logos, products and services. I thank you for it Father, Amen

Father God, I pray for the monetization of all my brands, logos, products and services. I pray for fearlessness and the ability to engage in analyzed skillful risk taking while completing profitable business transactions. I pray for the protection of my business and all of my brands from any counterfeit activity, fraudulent activity or harmful activity.

Heavenly Father, I pray for a competent and anointed team of Christian advisors, employees, independent contractors, business advisors and legal advisors that will provide wise counsel to assist me in the success of my business. I pray for the supernatural, exponential growth of my business.

Most importantly, I pray that the products and services that my business provides will be infused with the Power of the Holy Spirit and will positively impact the lives of everyone that purchases them. Amen

Prayer of Wealth Building

As Kingdom Heirs, God has given us the power to get wealth! Deuteronomy 8: 18 tells us "But thou shalt remember the LORD thy God: for *it is* he that giveth thee power to get wealth, that he may establish his covenant which he sware unto thy fathers, as *it is* this day." Wealth Building is not to be postponed, overlooked or ignored. Let's Pray!

Father God, in the Name of Jesus, I pray for the return of all the wealth that I would have built had I implemented wealth building strategies in the past. Your word says in Joel 2:25 "And I will restore to you the years that the locust hath eaten, the cankerworm, and the caterpillar, and the palmerworm, . . ." I pray for strategies and information to build wealth through business ownership, through investing in businesses owned by others, through real estate investing and through investing in the stock market. Amen

Abba Father, I pray for the unveiling of new untapped opportunities to build wealth. I pray for wealth building strategies in multiple countries and multiple currencies. I pray for the ability to accumulate and store wealth in multiple countries and multiple currencies. I pray for wealth building knowledge as it relates to investing in precious metals, such as gold.

Heavenly Father, I pray for wealth building knowledge as it relates to investing in new technologies of the future, including alternate currencies, digital systems and artificial intelligence. Most importantly, I pray that the wealth that I build using your supernatural strategies will grow exponentially and serve as a storehouse of generational wealth for my family. I pray this wealth will be used to finance and achieve the dreams, aspirations and business goals of the next generation of my family. Amen

Prayer of Favor & Influence

As Kingdom Heirs, God takes pleasure in giving us the Kingdom, however, he wants us to walk in wisdom and be good stewards with what he gives us. "For thou, LORD, wilt bless the righteous; with favour wilt thou compass him as *with* a shield" Psalm 5:12. We are surrounded by favor and our favor gives us the ability to impact the lives of others in a positive way. Let's pray!

Father God, in the Name of Jesus, I pray for activation of the favor you have already given me. I pray that your favor will envelop my entire life. I pray the favor on my life will cause me to receive preferential treatment, exclusive opportunities, invitations to events, meetings and gatherings where financial and contractual negotiations are conducted, settled and paid to me and my business in the form of cash, newly discovered opportunities, brand promotion and business advertisement. Amen

Abba Father, I pray for activation of the influence you have already given me. May my influence assist me in prospering in ministry, in business and in my personal life.
I pray that supernatural influence will follow me all the days of my life. I pray the influence I carry will cause others to pour knowledge, time, wealth, resources and opportunity into my life. May my influence go before me to reserve my seat at tables where financial prosperity is being negotiated and distributed.

Lord may my influence attract people to your word and to your ways. Let my life be a living testimony of your great works as your word instructs us in Matthew 5:16, "Let your light so shine before men, that they may see your good works, and glorify your Father which is in heaven." I pray the favor and influence that is upon my life will perpetually produce growth for your Kingdom. Amen

CONCLUSION

POSH PROTOCOL Volume III PRAYERS OF THE KINGDOM HEIR is Your Go-To Guide for developing a closer relationship with the Lord through prayer. Allow your spirit to connect directly with the Holy Spirit through the use of your Heavenly Language and begin to operate in supernatural power and revelation.

"Be careful for nothing; but in everything by prayer and supplication with thanksgiving let your requests be made known unto God. And the peace of God, which passeth all understanding, shall keep your hearts and minds through Christ Jesus." Philippians 4:6-7

~~~

If you have not yet accepted Jesus Christ as your personal Lord and Savior, Salvation is available to you today. *Simply turn the page,* believe and pray the Prayer of Salvation.

"...if thou shalt confess with thy mouth the Lord Jesus, and shalt believe in thine heart that God raised him from the dead, thou shalt be saved."

Romans 10:9

Prayer of Salvation

Heavenly Father, I confess I am a sinner. I repent of my sins. I believe your son Jesus Christ died for my sins. He was raised from the dead and He is alive right now. I accept Jesus Christ as my Lord and Savior now and forever. Lord, I surrender my life to you completely. Holy Spirit dwell within me and manifest your presence within me through an impartation of my own spoken heavenly language. Amen

Disclaimer

While the author and publisher have used their best efforts in preparing this book, they make no representations with respect to the accuracy or completeness of the contents of this book and specifically disclaim any implied warranties.

The material contained herein is for general information purposes. The author, publisher and all affiliates accept no responsibility and exclude all liability in connection with the use or application of the information contained herein. Words or phrases followed by the trademark symbols ™ or ® are the trademarked property of the author.

The brand name Dr. Posh® does not denote a doctoral or medical degree. The brand name Dr. Posh® is connotative of C.C. Preston's competence in Posh Protocol™, Christian Etiquette and Advocacy.

References

The Holy Bible, King James Version

ABOUT THE AUTHOR

C.C. Preston, branded as Dr. Posh® is The Posh Protocol Specialist

C.C. Preston, Dr. Posh® is a woman after God's own heart.

The Speaker, Entrepreneur and Minister is also the author of Posh *Protocol Volume 1: The 10 Commandments of Christian Accouterment For Women* and *Posh Protocol Volume 2*: Being Presidential

All the Glory belongs to God!